Little People, BIG DREAMS®

CHRIS HOY

Written by
Maria Isabel Sánchez Vegara

Illustrated by
Edita Hajdu

Frances Lincoln
Children's Books

TICKETS

This is the story of a boy from Edinburgh, Scotland, named Chris. When he was six, his parents took him to the cinema to see *E.T.* But what thrilled him most wasn't the alien in the film – it was the boy's amazing BMX bike. It could even fly!

Chris got his first bike from a jumble sale. It was old, but his dad fixed it up, painted it black and added cool stickers to make it special. Before long, Chris was zooming over ramps made of bricks and planks in the garden.

At seven Chris started racing. Every weekend he and his dad travelled across the country, making friends along the way. Chris wasn't the fastest, but the harder he tried, the better he got, until he finally earned his first victory.

HA-HA

So MUDDY!

FINALLY A WIN!

One day, Chris watched in awe as a Scottish cyclist zoomed around a smooth, indoor track. He wondered what it would feel like to ride that fast! But he kept racing over dirt tracks and jumps for six years, before making the switch to that shiny floor.

Chris loved the velodrome! It was like a huge, round bowl made for high-speed races.

He practised hard to master the kilo,
a race where a cyclist rides alone against the clock.
It wasn't long before he became a world champion.

In Athens, Chris pedalled faster than anyone before and won an Olympic gold medal.

But when the kilo race was dropped from the next Games, Chris trained hard to take on sprinting. It was a short, super-fast race, head-to-head against other cyclists.

Four years later, Chris took on three thrilling sprint events and conquered them all, becoming the first British athlete in a century to earn three gold medals at a single Olympics. Many would have stepped away after that, but not Chris.

GREAT

As he prepared for his final Olympics in London, Chris faced crashes, injuries and pressure to win. But one of his coaches, Steve, helped him think less about trophies and more about feeling calm and happy inside.

Every athlete dreams of ending their career with a victory in front of their home crowd. Winning his final race in London, Chris made history as the first Briton to earn six Olympic gold medals. And he got to celebrate with the whole country!

SO!!!
PROU
WELL
DONE!

After retiring, Chris didn't slow down. He raced cars, started a bike company, presented television shows and hosted a sports podcast. But nothing made him and his wife Sarra prouder than becoming the parents of Callum and Chloe.

One day Chris got some really tough news. He had an illness called cancer, and it couldn't be cured. Of course it wasn't easy, but he made the most of every day, finding joy and love even in the hardest moments.

Chris decided to share his story in a book, inspiring others to visit their doctors and take care of their health.

He also brought people together in a big bike ride to support those living with the same illness he had.

The great Chris Hoy – our little rider – kept pedalling, facing every obstacle with courage and kindness.

He showed the world that no matter how tough the road gets, we can turn every challenge into something meaningful.

CHRIS HOY

(Born 1976)

2002

2004

Chris Hoy was born in Edinburgh, Scotland. He began BMX racing aged seven and quickly learnt that the more he practised, the better he did. With hard work and determination, he became one of the UK's best young riders. He was a teenager when he discovered velodrome-track cycling. In 1996, he joined the British squad and three years later won his first World Championship medal – a silver in the team sprint. In 2002, his dream of becoming world champion came true when he won both the kilo time trial (by just 0.001 of a second!) and the team sprint. For the next ten incredible years, Chris won a medal at every World Championship and every Olympic Games, apart from in 2009 when he was injured. Race after race, he showed not only skill but also mental toughness.

2008

2024

At the Olympics in 2004, the three riders before him all broke the world kilo record, one after another. Undaunted, Chris simply went out and rode even faster, setting a new world record and winning gold! Perhaps Chris's greatest achievement came in 2008, when he won three gold medals at the Beijing Olympics. He was knighted the following year. When the Olympics came to London in 2012, Sir Chris finished off his amazing career in the best possible way, with two more gold medals. After he retired, he took on one of the world's toughest motorsports races, the Le Mans 24 Hours. In 2023, Chris was diagnosed with cancer. He raised awareness of the disease, making a huge difference to others. One of the greatest cyclists of all time, Chris will always be one of Britain's most-loved sporting heroes.

Want to find out more about **Chris Hoy**?

With the help of an adult, you can watch some of Chris's medal-winning races online.

Maria Isabel Sánchez Vegara has waived her royalty from the sale of this copy in recognition of the donation to Maggie's.

Original idea of the series by Maria Isabel Sánchez Vegara, published by Alba Editorial, s.l.u.
"Little People, BIG DREAMS" and "Pequeña & Grande" are trademarks of Alba Editorial s.l.u. and/or Beautifool Couple S.L.
First published in the UK and US in 2025 by Frances Lincoln Children's Books, an imprint of The Quarto Group.
1 Triptych Place, London, SE1 9SH, United Kingdom. T 020 7700 6700 **www.Quarto.com**
EEA Representation, WTS Tax d.o.o., Žanova ulica 3, 4000 Kranj, Slovenia. www.wts-tax.si

This book is not authorised, licensed or approved by Chris Hoy.
Any faults are the publisher's who will be happy to rectify for future printings.
A catalogue record for this book is available from the British Library.
ISBN 978-1-80570-041-8
Set in Futura BT.

Published by Peter Marley · Edited by Lucy Menzies
Designed by Sasha Moxon, Izzy Bowman and Karissa Santos
Editorial management by Izzie Hewitt
Production by Robin Boothroyd

Manufactured in Grude, Bosnia and Herzegovina
1 3 5 7 9 8 6 4 2

Photographic acknowledgements (pages 28-29, from left to right): 1. Chris Hoy of Scotland celebrates after winning the gold medal in the Men's 1000 m time trial final at the National Cycling centre during the 2002 Commonwealth Games in Manchester, England, on 28th July, 2002. 2. Olympic Games in Athens, 19th August, 2004. Chris Hoy wins the 100 m trial. 3. Triple Olympic gold medallist Chris Hoy parades on an open-top bus on 27th August, 2008, in Edinburgh, Scotland. Hundreds of people lined the Royal Mile to welcome back the medal-winning Olympians. 4. Sir Chris Hoy in the royal box during Wimbledon on 6th July, 2024, in London, England.

Collect the *Little People*, **BIG DREAMS**® series:

Scan the QR code for free activity sheets, teachers' notes and more information about the series at www.littlepeoplebigdreams.com